D0349591

~Colin Allbrook's~
NORTH DEVON

HALSGROVE

First published in 2002 by Halsgrove
© 2002 Colin Allbrook

*All rights reserved. No part of this publication may be reproduced,
stored in a retrieval system, or transmitted in any form or by any means
without the prior permission of the copyright holder.*

British Library Cataloguing-in-Publication Data
A CIP record for this title is available from the British Library

ISBN 1 84114 189 5

HALSGROVE
Halsgrove House
Lower Moor Way
Tiverton, Devon EX16 6SS
T: 01884 243242
F: 01884 243325
www.halsgrove.com

Printed in Hong Kong by Regal Printing

❧ *Contents* ❧

*This book is dedicated to my wife Chris and
my children, Juliet, Alice and Tom who
have filled my world with light and laughter*

∽ *Introduction* ∽

When I was eighteen and travelling each day on the underground to the centre of London I would see the same people, making the same journey to the same job. Some were young like me while others looked as if they had travelled that route for many years. I knew then that this was not for me and that one day I would have to do something else. Today, looking out of the studio window at the hill opposite, with the sheep grazing in the glow of the evening sun, I am pretty sure I made the right choice.

My life began in rather different circumstances at 9.20am on 8 March 1954 in Barnet, Hertfordshire, in my parents' bedroom with the midwife in attendance. I was the third child, with a sister Wendy born six years earlier, and a brother Barry who was three years older and suffering from chicken pox. This he apparently shared with his new brother and, 'Don't say I never give you anything' has been his cry ever since. Two years later another sister, Patricia, joined us and our rather cramped house was full. It was here in this small, three-bedroom, end-of-terrace house I was to live for the next twenty-one years. Although money was always in short supply we all seemed to survive quite happily.

To the rear of the house at the bottom of the garden was the local grammar school playing field, while to the front were several acres of woodland which eventually ran down to the park. Endless days were spent here, playing in amongst the trees and fields. Summers, which in my memory were always hot and sunny, were spent climbing trees and building camps, making dams across the local Pymes brook, which we then attempted to blow apart with bangers, learning to smoke and eventually to kiss. My enjoyment and love of the countryside of Devon today was, I think, formed during those early years in and around the woods and parks of Barnet.

'Art' in some form or other always ran through my childhood and was considered an important part of life. My father was a fine cello player and I believe he harboured ambitions of playing profession-ally at one time. His mother played the piano, while his father, as well as playing the 'fiddle', was a competent Sunday painter – as the walls of his house in Kingston bore testament. My mother, although unable to play any instrument, had a great love of music and was often able to name a piece after hearing just the first few bars. I have memories of classical music, especially Grieg's Piano Concerto, wafting around the house after we had bought our first gramophone player.

Marks from my primary school reports from these early years show I was enjoying art and getting good grades for my drawing and painting. I was, however, badly let down by my inability to spell correctly or tackle arithmetic, failings which today are sadly still the case.

As I grew older, school holidays involved a little more work as by now my father ran his own landscape and garden design business.

92 Daneland, Barnet, Hertfordshire, the house where I was born.

My brother often used to help with the work and I started in a small way to do a little labouring. Grass-cutting, helping with building and constructing walls and patios and even digging one or two graves were all part of the day, and while my brother took to it and carries on today as a landscape designer, I realised it was not for me. Drawing and painting was where my interest lay.

At about the age of thirteen I started to take this side of my life more seriously, deciding I wanted to work for myself, eventually earning a living as an artist. Originally I saw myself as a cartoonist and in 1968 I wrote to one of the greatest of them all, Giles, who was then working for the *Daily Express*. He replied wishing me luck and suggested I learn something of the processes involved in publishing. This I duly did and later this was to stand me in good stead when I entered the world of commercial art.

The secondary school I attended in Southgate, North London, had an excellent art teacher who was not only knowledgeable but also sympathetic to my ambitions. As I approached 'O' levels he taught me a great deal, even arranging for me to attend evening classes at a college in Hackney where he taught a couple of times a week. Life, however, was not all drawing and as a member of the local Scout group I also spent those teenage years camping, hill walking, learning to sail and canoe, caving and much else besides. There were opportunities to travel abroad to Europe as well. I visited Spain, hiked in France, went with a group of friends in an old coach round Holland and Belgium and drove across Germany with my brother and another couple of friends. The Scout group also put on an annual review and here I had my first taste of designing backdrops and scenery for the stage.

The 'O' level exams came and went and I managed somehow to gain six, and also sell my first paintings. At school we had an exhibition of coursework produced over the year and the French teacher bought two of my pieces, a pencil drawing of a still life and a painting, for the princely sum of £2 I think. So now I was definitely on my way!

I decided to stay on at school and study both art and history at 'A' level. At this time the school was in its final year as a boys' school before becoming a mixed comprehensive, and a certain amount of freedom was evident. This I was able to adapt to my own ends so after a couple of months I dropped history and just concentrated on my art. I was now free to spend every day hidden away in the artroom, drawing, painting and experimenting with different techniques and media. I was also encouraged to visit exhibitions in local galleries and museums, which meant I was exposed to a greater range of artwork. Overall it was a bit like doing a foundation year at an art college and I loved it.

It was in 1971 during this first year of 'A' levels that I was introduced to the neighbour of an old school friend of my father's, a fine watercolourist named Ken Langstaff. The commercial art studio where he worked as an illustrator was looking for a messenger and it was suggested I apply for the job. I was offered an interview, which I attended clutching a portfolio of my work. They liked what they saw and I was offered a week's trial in June after which the job was mine, starting as soon as possible. I was only one year into the two-year course but it was decided that I should take my 'A' level a year early and so this I did. I achieved a grade A in the exam and left school, taking with me the art prize for that year, to start work in London's West End in a studio on the fifth floor of a building in Shaftesbury Avenue. I was paid £7 a week, rising to £9 after two months, and for the next four years I stayed with the studio, travelling each day by tube to Leicester Square.

I can still remember the distinctive smell that pervaded the studio, largely due to the glue we used for pasting up artwork. This was a product known as Cow Gum, the odour of which pervaded everything, and as it was a petrol-based substance probably accounted for the slightly zany people you encountered in studios such as these. Seeing the professional artwork produced in the studio for the first time, however, was quite daunting. There was immaculately produced hand-lettering, beautiful illustrations of packages or bottles and my favourites, the book illustrations for a children's annual. The studio used to produce this annual for one of its clients, the Royal Society for the Prevention of Accidents or ROSPA. It was called the *Tufty Annual* and concerned the adventures of a red squirrel named Tufty, and all his friends, who were used to highlight the dangers of crossing the road or playing in dangerous places. Ken used to produce most of the illustrations, which he painted in watercolour, and he brought to these drawings a knowledge gained from long study with pencil, paper and brush in the countryside. At last I did a few pages myself and it was a great thrill the first time I saw the published result.

Over my time at the studio I learnt all aspects of the commercial art business, from typesetting to design and layout, but it was to illustration that I gravitated. As well as producing illustrations of bottles of Lucozade and for road-safety posters I have also drawn and painted the blackcurrants and leaves seen on the label of a bottle of Ribena!

During the first couple of years working here I also attended St Martin's School of Art a couple of evenings a week where I studied life drawing. We were lucky usually to have two or three models in attendance, from ballerinas to a large 'Rubenesque' lady, and these studies taught me a great deal about drawing the human form.

In the life class I usually drew in pencil or charcoal but at the studio most of the illustration work was produced in both pen and ink or watercolour. It was here by watching and using the paint I learnt the technique of handling watercolours and finding out the medium's capabilities. Today, even though I frequently work in all of the different media, I think watercolour is still my first love.

With this growing confidence in handling watercolour I was also painting and exhibiting locally in North London. Often these were paintings of the human figure and it was usually my girlfriend Christine who was persuaded to pose for me. The art critic of the local paper wrote of one of my pictures in 1977:

Colin Allbrook is showing a lovely watercolour of a reclining girl – indeed that is the title. This is a most delicate yet sure work. Everything in its place and nothing superfluous. A really satisfying piece of art.

He must have meant it as he bought the painting and commissioned a companion piece to hang with it!

Owing to the electricity shutdowns in the mid-seventies, a shorter working week was introduced throughout England and so for one day a week, in my case Friday, I worked at home. This gave me a taste for being at home and working how and when I pleased. Coincidentally Chris and I had a fortnight's holiday in Cornwall, and sitting on the cliffs overlooking the Atlantic, we decided we would like to leave Hertfordshire when the time was right and perhaps move to the South West. I decided to hand my notice in at the studio and work freelance so, with a month's wages and understanding parents behind me, I started to work from home. I was twenty-one years old and that was the last time I was to have a 'proper' job. The family had by now moved to a different area of Barnet to a bigger house. My eldest sister was long-since married and my younger

sister away nursing so there was rather more space than there had been previously. I set up my drawing board on the dining-room table and until 1979 this was where I worked.

I started doing freelance work for my old studio and for various print and stationery companies, as well as painting and exhibiting. One day a week I worked as a paste-up artist for a local free paper. This paper consisted mainly of adverts, which, being still the days before computers, were all made up by hand; the typesetting, done on an electric typewriter, was pasted up manually, along with any relevant illustration or logo, into boarders of the correct size. These adverts were then stuck up together as complete pages, photographed, retouched to remove blemishes and delivered by carrier to the printer. He then printed the paper overnight and sent it out the next morning for distribution. I started work at nine o'clock in the morning, laying out the type and producing the odd illustration as required, and finished whenever the paper was complete, sometimes at two o'clock the following morning. Nowadays, with the whole of the publishing industry transformed by the advent of computers, this would no longer happen and the paper would be produced in a fraction of the time.

In 1979 Chris and I decided to get married and then, at last, we moved from Barnet to set up home in the West Country, on the outskirts of Ilfracombe. As we had thought about this earlier when we were in Cornwall it seemed the ideal time to make the break. I knew Devon from family holidays and we also had friends in the area so it seemed a good place to settle. Chris is a nurse and as such was able to obtain a job pretty easily and I, as a freelance artist, could work anywhere. I have subsequently discovered that my great-grandmother was from the West, having been born in the village of Monkton Combe just outside Bath, so perhaps there was a subconscious connection.

In our terraced cottage I graduated from the dining-room table to the heady heights of the third small bedroom which now became my first studio. By now I was sending and selling my work to publishers throughout the country and this was to continue. Locally, I joined the art society and my paintings were sold in the large summer exhibition they held in the town. This in turn led to galleries locally requesting my work to exhibit and sell.

Up to this point I had painted mainly figure studies and landscapes but this approach was about to change. On a trip back from

Hertfordshire we stopped off at a farm in Somerset and bought some apples. As the box lay on the table at home later, the apples spilling out, I noticed how the light affected the subject. I produced a watercolour and exhibited in an open show at the Brewhouse in Taunton and although it did not sell it taught me to look for subjects in a different way. Suddenly I could see paintings everywhere and I realised you did not have to go out looking for subjects to paint. I started painting still life, perhaps a cider jar or maybe a rocking chair, but the way the light lit the object bought it to life. As my wife performed everyday tasks around the house I also painted her, but informally, not posed as previously. The light in the house filtering through the windows transformed these actions into something special. As the artist John Constable wrote, 'You never have to add life to a scene, for if you sit quietly and wait, life will come.' I have found this to be the case so often, especially these days when painting on farms or in the markets.

The first of our children, Juliet, was born in 1984 and this I found opened up another avenue to explore and paint. From those early days of seeing her being fed or sleeping in her cot, I drew and painted her.

Then in 1986, with my wife pregnant again, we decided to move as we needed more space. After a search we found a house in the beautiful Taw Valley at Umberleigh. Set in the woods it looks out across the river and the valley beyond and although it was not ideal, having both steep steps and garden, something we vowed we did not want again, we fell in love with it and bought it. Just over two months later our second daughter, Alice, was born. I now had two of them to paint and, with the arrival of our son, Tom, in 1992, I have continued to find them a constant source of ideas and inspiration. As with all children they were never still for very long so I followed them with a sketchbook, constantly drawing. This gives you not only the ability to work fast but also teaches you to catch the essence of a pose concisely and in a very short space of time. When I later started working in the theatre I found this experience very useful. Nowadays they are around less but I still draw them, Juliet with her dancing, Alice her horse riding and Tom on the beach, perhaps, or swimming in the river.

I now decided it was time to send some work to a London show so in 1987 I submitted some paintings to the summer show of the Royal Watercolour Society. These were accepted and sold and this marked the beginning for me of regularly showing in London with various art societies. The following year I won fourth prize in the Royal Bath & West exhibition at Shepton Mallet for a painting of logs in a shed, again confirming my belief that one can paint ordinary simple things. Prizes like these can be a great boost to your confidence and I have gone on twice to win the first prize, and this year (2002) second prize, at the same show for paintings showing similar subject matter.

Success of the same kind came my way in London, too, where I won the Daler-Rowney award at the Royal Watercolour Society. This was for a painting I did of Juliet and Alice playing Scrabble on the lounge floor, and this is now housed in the Daler-Rowney collection. As a result of winning this prize I was invited to spend a day at the Bankside Gallery in Blackfriars demonstrating watercolour techniques to the public alongside artists such as Leslie Worth and Tom Coates. I admire the work they both produce so it was great to learn something of how they approach their painting.

The early nineties saw me become unofficial artist in residence at the Queen's Theatre in Barnstaple. In 1991 Juliet was chosen to dance in the pantomime at the theatre. Whilst waiting to pick her up after the endless rehearsals I started to make some drawings and became interested in the possibilities presented by the performers and the lighting. After a few enquiries I was given permission to stand and draw from the wings during the performance, a practice I still continue today when I can. When the theatre closed for refurbishment I was invited to record the construction, so wearing a hard hat and with pencil and chalk, I spent many days drawing as the theatre took shape. This resulted in an exhibition of these drawings and paintings at the gala opening in 1994. I have carried on working at the Queen's Theatre ever since, drawing everyone from Rolf Harris and Chris Barber to the English National Ballet Company. It was as a result of working here that I was commissioned to design some sets for the European Ballet Company. They are a touring company who have visited Barnstaple on a number of occasions and while working on stage during a performance I was introduced to their director, ex-Bolshoi dancer Stanislav Tchassov. He asked if I was interested in producing some designs for them and as a result I have worked on several ballets including the Nutcracker and Cinderella. Little did I think when designing backdrops for the Scout shows that thirty years later I would do the same for a professional ballet company.

Throughout the 1990s I continued to exhibit each year with several of the professional art societies that are members of the Federation of British Artists, based at the Mall Galleries in London. The Royal

My studio at Umberleigh.

Institute of Painters in Watercolour, the Pastel Society, the Royal Society of Painters in Oils and the Royal Society of Marine Artists have all shown my work regularly, reflecting my interest and use of the various media.

Living in Umberleigh we have several friends and neighbours who live and work on farms. My interest in painting interiors at home led me to search for larger spaces to paint and so I ended up in some of these places. Here I spent time in old barns and sheds with their beautiful dusty light often filtered through dirty windows festooned with cobwebs. Again it was the ordinary daily chores, milking or feeding, that caught my eye and this has provided me with endless pictures. A friend, a member of the Society of Equestrian Artists, seeing these, some of which included stables and horses, suggested I send some work to the Society's annual show held at Christie's in London. This I did and had the work accepted and continued to do so each year. I was elected an Associate of the Society and a full member in 1998. Our president, until his death, was the well-known painter Terence Cuneo and each year he presented an award at the exhibition. In 1999 I was very pleased to receive this, the Cuneo Medal, for the most outstanding group of paintings.

Another award came my way in 1999 at the Royal Institute of Painters in Watercolour. It was the award for the best use of light in a painting, which in this case, was of a local farmer working the grain dryer in one of his sheds. Talking later to one or two of the members it was suggested I apply for membership of the society which I subsequently did the following year. In 2001 my fellow artists elected me a full member and as one of only 65 members I was delighted with the honour. This now allows me to hang six paintings at the Institute's annual show in the Mall Galleries.

The Swiss painter Paul Klee said of art that it didn't reproduce the visible but rather it made it visible, and by continuing to paint the ordinary things of life, the lambing shed, a cattle auction or perhaps someone repairing a boat, that's what I would like to achieve. Last year at the Royal West of England Academy I was given an award for a painting of Holsworthy market; this year at the Royal Bath & West Show my study of sheep shearers at South Molton market took second prize. I think that, hopefully, this shows the things that continue to excite and inspire me will and can be enjoyed by others.

Colin at work

~Painting Methods~

Watercolour, which was the technique I was first taught, is I think, my favourite of all the different media. However, I also work frequently in oil and pastels and find this switching between the different materials helps keep the work lively as each presents me with a different set of problems.

My usual method of working is to stand and make pencil or charcoal drawings with colour notes or sometimes produce oil or watercolour studies. These I use to produce the finished painting at home in the studio where one has more time to consider and arrange the composition. Often, though, I will produce a complete painting on the spot.

WATERCOLOUR

Watercolour can be an unpredictable medium but the spontaneity of the marks made make it exhilarating to use. I love the work of past masters such as John Singer Sargeant for his vigorous use of paint and today, the watercolours of Leslie Worth for their beautiful execution. It is a medium I find superb for portraying the soft atmospheric light of an interior with its subtle colours and tones.

My preferred paper is handmade and comes from a mill in Somerset. It is called 'Two Rivers' and can be bought in three or four different colours, my favourites being the cream and green though lately I have been using the white. The weight is about 175gms and I always stretch the paper as I love the quality it gives when painting on it.

If the subject is complex I may draw it first in pencil which I then lift from the paper with a rubber so only a faint line remains, or indicate it with a brush. Recently though I haven't used either but started straight in with washes.

I usually begin by flooding the paper with paint, broadly indicating in an abstract way, the different tones and colours. This I allow to dry and then gradually lay washes, one over another, strengthening the tone here or there until the image begins to emerge from the paper.

Sometimes I mix a little gouache with the watercolour and drop this into a wash, which gives it a lovely chalky bloom. 'Bodycolour' as this combination is known, I use for highlighting in the final stages which as a result of working on tinted paper, really sings out. A bristle brush, clean water and a piece of paper towel can also be used to create these highlights.

When working outside I usually prefer to use pans of watercolour in a box as they are easily transportable but in the studio I favour tubes of paint usually Winsor & Newton artists colours. The colours I use, tend to be roughly the same whether painting in watercolour, oils or even pastel, though here a greater range is needed because of the inability to mix them in the same way as other media.

The colours that make up my palette are:

Cerulean blue
Prussian blue
Payne's grey
Windsor violet
Cadmium red
Cadmium yellow
yellow ochre
sap green
burnt umber
burnt sienna

I also use, as mentioned earlier, a white gouache that I prefer to Chinese White as this I find a little thin. One or two others may be included from time to time but usually it is these nine or ten colours.

OIL

I apply oils either on stretched canvas or on MDF board, and this I prime with a mixture of clear gesso and PVA glue, which gives the surface of the board texture and interest. I also treat grey pulp board (cardboard) in this way which then has a lovely absorbent quality that allows me to work quickly without a build-up of paint or the surface becoming slippery.

Using a turpentine/linseed oil mixture (50/50) the main areas are drawn in loosely and the tones broadly indicated. Gradually these

tones and colours are built up across the picture surface, concentrating on the overall look rather than on any one area. As the picture progresses sharper details are added, refining the painting until a certain point is reached and it feels finished. When you are adding marks for their own sake rather than developing the picture any further, you know you have reached this stage.

The painting is then left in the studio over the next few days where, frequently,

I look at it and adjust any colour that needs altering or any tone that requires strengthening.

PASTEL

In a life class I will often work with pastel in front of the figure but, as with the other media, I often rely on my studies and drawings to produce a painting.

The surface I use is either Ingres paper or cardboard treated the same way as for the oil painting, with gesso and PVA glue. This gives the finished pastel a lively and interesting surface. The initial drawing is laid in using either a harder pastel or a piece of charcoal, pencil being no good for this as it does not cover at all well with pastel. Then, as with the paintings in the other media, the whole surface is worked as one, blocking in the colours and tones lightly at first and then, as different areas become established, laying the pastel more positively. By working this way the pastel does not become too thick early on and this allows for easy adjustment. Gradually, as the work progresses, the picture emerges from within the surface.

I tend to use a greater range of colours because, as stated earlier, the problem of mixing the pastel. You can't! The colours have to be mixed on the picture by laying strokes of colour one over another and the resulting juxtaposition of colours can be very exciting. You can, of course, mix them by rubbing one colour into another but I find the colours become very dead and lifeless this way. One of the great things about a finished pastel is its surface with the mass of marks and broken colour.

There are usually 150 or so different colours in a range of pastels but in practice many of these are four or five tints of the same colour. With a cobalt blue, for instance, you could have a tint 0 which is very pale or a tint 6 which would be quite a bit stronger. I tend to have two or three tints of the same colour rather than three different colours as this keeps the painting more harmonious.

I use the harder pastels such as Conte for the initial stages and then move to a softer Unison pastel as the work progresses, often finishing the work with the even softer Daler/Rowney pastels. The use of fixative is kept to the very minimum as this tends to darken the pastel if used too heavily. I then either frame the end result or store the pictures flat between sheets of newspaper which, as long as the paper does not move, will prevent them smudging.

The Paintings

ℒFarms and Markets℘

Living in a farming community I suppose it was inevitable I would eventually use this as material for my paintings. I loved painting figures in interior spaces and when looking for subjects like this I ended up on some of these farms. The old barns and even the newer sheds have a lovely quality of light to them and there is nearly always activity of some kind going on in and around them.

Most of the farm paintings featured in the book are based on work produced locally at the homes of friends and neighbours. George and Pauline Warne at Emmett, James and Jill Waldren at Court Farm, and Colin and Jayne Heard at Eastacott, have all allowed me to wander freely around their places of work and been generous with their time explaining the different activities, and I thank them very much for that.

I love working in these places with their clutter of machinery, sacks, boxes and livestock. The light, often coming from high up through roof lights or perhaps half-doors lower down, is filtered through dust and cobwebs and the straw reflects it back in ochre greens illuminating the dark corners or perhaps someone working. Sometimes the buildings are viewed from outside, maybe standing in the yard on a winter evening during milking or lambing. Then the electric light glows warmly from the shed and contrasts with cool colours outside.

Working on the farms has led me in turn to produce some drawings at several of the livestock markets in North Devon, mainly South Molton, Barnstaple and Holsworthy. Again the activity of the sales in and around the pens was interesting and I have produced many paintings on the subject. Sadly since the outbreak of Foot and Mouth the access is understandably more restricted than previously and some of these scenes I would be unable to draw now. Indeed some have been lost for ever as markets such as Barnstaple livestock market have now ceased.

The old orchard, Emmett
Oil 24 x 36in

Taw Valley cattle, Newbridge
Oil 16 x 20in

The feeders had been placed under these trees during the autumn, so the cattle tended to collect there a lot of the time. I drove by several times and when the light was right I stopped and made some notes. To get the light shining through the trees I had to clamber up a bank into a hedge, which was a little awkward.

Devon farmyard
Oil 12 x 10in

Orchard cattle
Oil 14 x 18in

February milking, Eastacott
Oil   10 x 12in

Sheep on the hill
Oil 10 x 12in

The farm dogs
Watercolour & bodycolour 14 x 20in

The dogs at George and Pauline's farm are always wandering around, racing after the tractor or quad bike as it leaves the yard. Here they are in quieter mood, resting in the sun, for although it was only January there was some warmth to be had.

Candy in the barn
Oil 20 x 24in

Lambing shed, February
Oil 20 x 30in

Lambing time, Emmett
Watercolour & bodycolour 14 x 21in

Market shearers, South Molton
Oil 16 x 20in

Before the Foot and Mouth outbreak I drew these shearers as they worked in South Molton market. Owing to hygiene regulations the sheep had to be partially clipped to clean them up which was done as they were unloaded. Since the epidemic this part of the market is no longer used and I am not sure if it will be again. I sent this painting to the exhibition at the Royal Bath & West Show this year where it was awarded the second prize.

Sheep sale, Holsworthy market
Oil 16 x 20in

Last sun, January farmyard
Watercolour & bodycolour 13 x 20in

Cattle in the wood, Cuttam copse
Oil 32 x 40in

Spring cows
Oil 14 x 18in

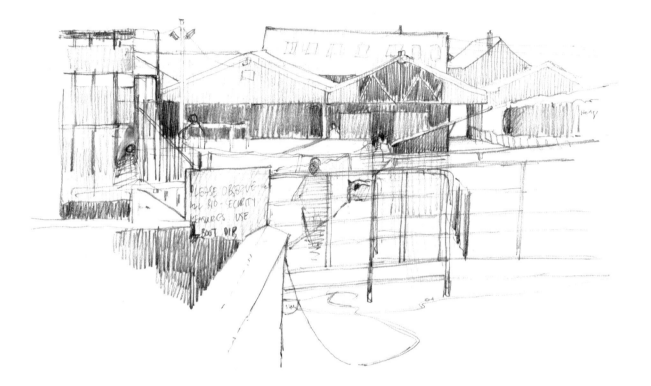

Red deer, Longdown Wood
Watercolour & bodycolour 20 x 28in

On the hill opposite the farmhouse at Emmett is this stand of pines which dominates the skyline. I was drawing in the field below the wood and the deer appeared. There had been a group of four seen around but somehow this one had become separated from the others and it trotted to and fro looking for them. I drew it as its silhouette broke the skyline below the dark mass of the pines.

33

First snow, South Molton market
Watercolour & bodycolour 13 x 18in

We had to drive to South Molton one day, to catch a bus. It was snowing as we left Umberleigh but by the time we reached town it was quite heavy and became heavier still as we waited for the bus. Being a Thursday, the livestock market was on and under a blanket of snow looked quite different. I had no painting equipment with me so I dashed into the art shop and bought a pencil and sketch-book. The snow virtually stopped and a watery sun started to break through, the warm patches of sunlight contrasting beautifully with the cool blue shadows of the snow.

Nocturne with rising moon, Newbridge
Oil 24 x 36in

As I drove across Newbridge, near Barnstaple, one evening this orange moon was just rising from behind the hill. I stopped and made some notes and this was the result. That time on the cusp of night when it is neither dark nor light, turns all the colours to these delicious mauves and blues. The river, which was running high, picked up the colour of the moon, as did the foreground puddles.

Checking the ewes
Watercolour & bodycolour 19 x 13in

This was the first lambing session of the year at Emmett and the ewes with their lambs were in the shed protected from the elements by the bales of straw. Millie the dog, however, was intent on annoying them as much as possible. She would creep nearer and nearer a pen until the ewe stamped its foot, at which point she barked and dashed off. The whole process was then repeated again.

Winter barn, Eastacott
Oil 20 x 30in

Taw Valley harvest
Watercolour & bodycolour 13 x 20in

Bartridge sheep
Watercolour & bodycolour 9 x 13in

In the shade
Watercolour & bodycolour 9 x 13in

The auctioneer, Barnstaple market
Pastel 11 x 8in

This pastel was made from a drawing I did at the weekly sheep sales in Barnstaple market. These were held each Friday when the sheep and cattle were brought in for the auction and the town filled with tractors and trailers as they were delivered. The town is still crowded on a Friday but the livestock market has gone so I don't suppose you will see a scene such as this again in Barnstaple.

The sheep market, South Molton
Watercolour & bodycolour 17 x 25in

Market day snow
Watercolour & bodycolour 13 x 20in

Sheep shearing, rolling the fleece
Pastel 14 x 20in

This was one of several paintings I did as a result of watching the sheep being sheared at a farm up the road. It was a boiling-hot day and the men sheared more than 300 sheep while I produced a lot of drawings. Mind you, I think they sweated a bit more than me!

The cattle auction, Holsworthy
Watercolour & bodycolour 7 x 11in

In the valley field, Emmett
Oil 14 x 18in

Morning mist at Newbridge
Oil 24 x 36in

As you cross Newbridge on the main road into Barnstaple the valley opens out into a broad flood plain. The morning mist spreads out across the fields and river and with a hazy sun showing, the whole valley is wreathed in light and mystery. Trees are half in focus and the cattle appear to float above the meadow, while the river sparkles as the sun breaks through a little.

Hens
Oil 10 x 8in

Working in the summer shed, Court Farm
Watercolour & bodycolour 13 x 19in

The farm dog, Court Farm
Watercolour & bodycolour 13 x 19in

Rare breeds show
Pastel 14 x 18in

In the cowshed
Oil 12 x 16in

Afternoon light
Oil 10 x 12in

The poultry show
Oil 10 x 12in

Market day in South Molton
Watercolour & bodycolour 13 x 19in

Barn interior
Watercolour & bodycolour 20 x 26in

✑ The Coastline and Sea ✑

The village of Instow sits on the estuary where the waters of the Taw and Torridge meet and make their way out to sea. This coastal village has become a favourite place of mine to paint and over the years I have produced many pictures of the area.

The view I love most is that looking down the estuary towards Bideford and the hills beyond. Here in Instow the opposite bank is dominated by the bulk of Appledore shipyard with its dual cranes. In the winter the channel below the yard is virtually empty, while in spring and summer it fills with craft of various shape and size lying at anchor. As the tide recedes these boats settle on the mud at different angles and when the sun shifts west the wet mud glistens and becomes a mass of blues and purples touched in places with gold, while the yard and hills beyond become a silhouette. On summer days the high tide brings the cadet dinghies out from the yacht club and their bright pink sails, along with those of other craft, add further colours to the scene.

On the other side of the quay the warmer months bring windbreaks and people to the beach and the whole place becomes a hive of activity and colour. Stand on the quay steps on a summer's evening and the reflections of the buildings in the sea are turned a rich gold by the sun and the shadowed walls, deep cool blues. This time of day in Instow, late afternoon and evening on a warm summer's day, is a time I love to gather material for paintings when all these rich colours and tones become so evident.

Evening light over Appledore
Oil 20 x 30in

Instow blue
Oil 20 x 24in

The tide has gone down and the boats sit on the glittering mud. The colours and tones of the wet mud are a great thing to paint and I never tire of doing so.

Beach boy
Oil 12 x 10in

Boatyard light
Oil 10 x 12in

The boats in the yard at North Devon Yacht Club, some being worked on while others are just parked up. The light, shapes and colours make an interesting subject and certainly worth painting.

Under the stern, Kathleen and May
Watercolour & bodycolour 26 x 19in

When this boat was being restored on Brunswick Wharfe in Bideford I managed to spend some time there drawing. While out of the water the hull made a fascinating subject to paint, especially with the scaffolding erected round it and the figures at work. The shiny black hull reflected the blue sky and the dusty ochre ground, while the scaffolding cast intricate shadows across everything. I think they made an excellent job of the restoration and would like to see the boat remain in Bideford.

Before the launch
Watercolour & bodycolour 13 x 20in

Dinghies in the estuary
Watercolour & bodycolour 14 x 20in

Working on the masts
Watercolour & bodycolour 13 x 20in

Restoration, Kathleen and May
Watercolour & bodycolour 19 x 26in

Instow Quay, late sun
Oil   20 x 30in

Working in the boatyard, yacht club
Oil 14 x 18in

Pink dusk in the estuary
Oil 8 x 14in

Appledore light
Oil 16 x 20in

Summer, Torridge estuary
Oil 20 x 30in

This was regatta day in Instow, the morning had been grey and overcast and the light very flat. As the day progressed, the racing finished and the tide receded, taking with it the cloud and leaving a glorious hot, sunny afternoon. Out came the windbreaks and the beach filled with people relaxing, while out in the water one or two dinghies tacked up and down, their sails triangles of light against the hills.

Lundy from Morte Point
Oil 32 x 40in

I paint a lot at Instow but had it in mind to do some paintings of other stretches of the coast. I knew Morte Point from my days living in Ilfracombe so decided to head for there. I sat on a cliff-top bench and did an oil study for this painting but had to stop after about forty minutes because of the constant buffeting by the wind. It was not particularly cold but it was very irritating. Still, I did enough to produce this picture and shall probably return to the area again.

Walkers on Baggy Point
Watercolour & bodycolour 20 x 28in

Blue light, Instow
Watercolour & bodycolour 9 x 13in

Instow sails
Oil 7 x 15in

~Ponies and the Moor~

Over the years I have often visited the moor to draw the ponies but the annual round-up in October is a good time to see them close at hand. I was invited to Knighton Farm at Withypool to see Korina Mitchell's herd when they were brought in for sorting and branding. It's a lovely sturdy little horse, the Exmoor, and great to paint. The colour that ranges from almost a deep orange to a much darker form is beautiful and the pale tone round the eye and muzzle really shows it off. Exmoor in autumn is full of these colours and the ponies match their surroundings perfectly.

Ponies near Hawkridge
Oil 10 x 20in

Branding shed, Exmoor
Watercolour & bodycolour 13 x 21in

One October I stayed with an artist friend in a cottage on Furzehill Common above Barbrook. He had come down to see the ponies brought in from the moor but the weather was not much good and we did not see a great deal. However, the owner of the cottage also ran a small herd of Exmoor ponies and these she brought into the shed to brand a couple of the youngsters. As pure-bred Exmoors they have to be registered and branded. The ponies did not seem to care for it too much but we managed to get some drawings of the horses, after all.

The sale, Knighton Farm
Oil 10 x 20in

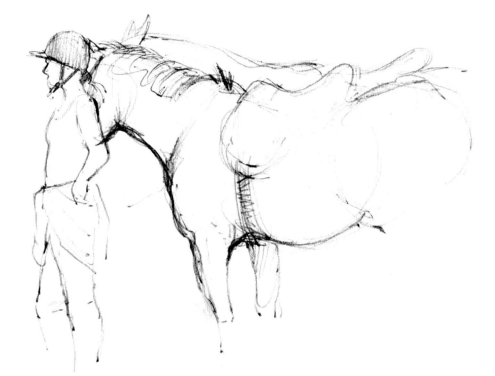

Ponies in the shade
Oil 12 x 16in

These Exmoor ponies are part of a small herd owned by neighbours down the road. They were grazing on the river-bank but the summer heat drove them into the shade, under the trees by the gate. I had spotted them there a few days before and when I went back to draw them, sure enough, they were back again in the cool.

The Bay
Watercolour & bodycolour 9 x 14in

October on the moor
Oil 10 x 14in

Riders on the moor above Simonsbath
Oil 12 x 16in

Staghounds, Brendon Two Gates
Oil 18 x 24in

❧ The Theatre and Dance ❧

Working in the theatre has often been a challenge as well as great fun. Standing in the wings, usually in bad light, one has to be constantly aware of people going on or coming off stage. The actors, musicians and dancers are rarely still for any length of time so I have had to learn to draw quickly.

Musicians tend to be the easiest to draw as they are relatively static for reasonable lengths of time and while they do move, they tend to return to their original positions frequently, allowing the drawing to progress. The most difficult are the dancers as they are never still, constantly and quickly changing position, so usually with the ballet I have to content myself with drawing them as they stand in the wings preparing to go on. However, if the company is appearing on successive nights it is often possible to add a little to the drawing each night until the sketch is complete.

Obviously different from working in the daylight, stage lighting gives some brilliant effects with vibrant colours such as reds, blues and purples and strong bright highlights. I love the halo of light made by the spotlight and the warm glow thrown up onto the performers from the stage as they stand in the wings, half lost in shadow. These are the things I look for to give the pictures a sense of atmosphere and anticipation.

The Saturday ballet class
Watercolour & bodycolour 21 x 16in

I spent some time in Juliet's ballet class on a Saturday making some drawings. It is held in a hall in Newport, Barnstaple, that has this marvellous window at one end, which illuminates the whole room. The scale and brightness of it make a good background against which to depict the dancers.

Tying her shoe
Oil 10 x 14in

The dancer, English Touring Ballet
Oil 24 x 30in

Waiting for the finale
Watercolour & bodycolour 16 x 21in

Here a collection of children, some dressed as rats, wait for their entrance to join the action on stage. It is the annual pantomime, *Dick Whittington*, which was performed at the Queen's Theatre. The warm shadows in the wings contrast with the brilliantly lit stage beyond.

Scaffolding on the balcony
Pastel 22 x 16in

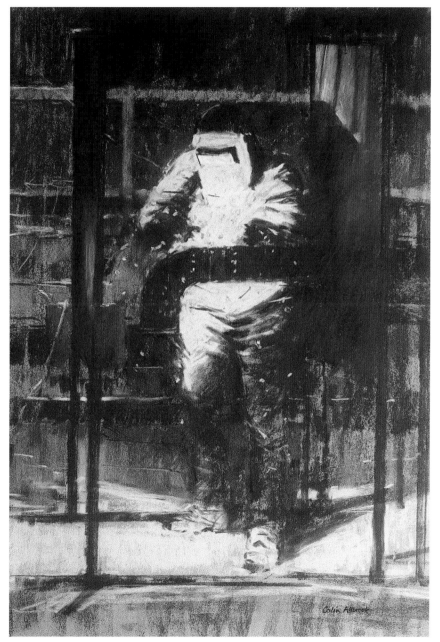

Arc welding, Queen's Theatre
Pastel 22 x 16in

Pete Allan Jazz Band
Watercolour & bodycolour 13 x 20in

Jaleo Flamenco
Pastel 28 x 20in

Fagin
Watercolour & bodycolour 17 x 13in

The rose dress
Pastel 12 x 16in

The bagpipe player
Oil 10 x 12in

The red tutu
Pastel 17 x 13in

This is Juliet in a red tutu that she wore for one of her dances. She loved putting it on and was easily persuaded to wear it so I could draw her.

Jake the Peg (Rolf Harris)
Conte pencil 12 x 7in

Rolf Harris appeared at the Queen's Theatre for a couple of nights and as part of his act performed his 'Jake the Peg' routine. I made this drawing in conte pencil while he went through his song.

Roy Hudd
Conte pencil 12 x 9in

Dance class study
Watercolour & bodycolour 8 x 6in

The panto dame
Pastel 20 x 14in

Evening recital
Charcoal & pastel 22 x 17in

The flute solo
Oil 24 x 48in

Kenny Ball
Oil 12 x 10in

The pianist
Pastel 16 x 20in

Waiting in the wings
Pastel 15 x 12ins

Sinfonietta
Charcoal & pastel 20 x 28in

⸺ Umberleigh and the River ⸺

The house in Umberleigh is set in an area of mixed woodland which in spring is full of daffodils and then a little later, blue-bells. There is plenty of wildlife with deer and foxes being frequent visitors to the garden. The hedges are full of birds and as dusk falls the tawny owls start calling from among the trees.

Below the house is the River Taw that runs on its way to the estuary seven or eight miles further on. The river rises on Dartmoor and the Devon rain, of which we have plenty, causes it to fill rapidly, only for it to drop back just as quickly when it stops. The water drops over a small weir opposite us so the sound of water is constant in the house.

Since moving here, the house, garden and river have featured in many of my paintings. The house faces east which means the morning sun floods the rooms and garden with light and I have frequently made drawings of Chris and the children at this time of day. The river also has been a great source for paintings with the sunlight sparkling on its surface and the deep green stretches of slower water as it moves into the shadow of the bank. It is this contrast of dark tones set against the more brightly lit areas that makes it so interesting to paint.

The painting shown overleaf is of a stretch of river in which count-less children have swum over the years. The picture was a commis-sion for friends of ours, Rob and Veronica, and is of a summer after-noon with our families down on the riverbank. The barbecue is alight and the sun has turned the trees and banks gold while the air is warm and drowsy. Sipping chilled white wine, watching the children play in the river, it is the perfect way to end the day.

Summer on the river
Oil 16 x 20in

Rising trout
Oil 16 x 24in

Afternoon sun
Oil 10 x 14in

The pool
Oil 10 x 14in

The bridge at Umberleigh
Oil 16 x 20in

Spring fisherman
Oil 18 x 24in

During the fishing season in spring the fishermen appear in the village. Often staying at the pub, they can be seen out on the river trying their luck in various places. This man I spotted as I walked along the bank, standing in the water above Umberleigh bridge. It was afternoon and the sun had shifted west above the hill and now shone through the fresh spring leaves in a vibrant glow of yellow.

September on the Taw, Umberleigh
Oil 12 x 16in

On the river bed
Oil 8 x 16in

Taw fisherman
Watercolour & bodycolour 11 x 8in

I was down on the river doing some water-colours when the fisherman appeared, so I painted him. It is so often the case if you sit and work a picture will present itself without having to seek it out.

Fishing, late afternoon, Taw
Oil   18 x 24in

Paddling in the river
Watercolour & bodycolour 10 x 13in

Autumn, River Taw
Oil 10 x 14in

August on the Taw
Oil 28 x 36in

Pumpkin moon
Oil 24 x 16in

Tom had a pumpkin that we had carved for a school's display at Rosemoor gardens. When we lit the candle inside it gave this lovely yellow glow. A moon rose opposite the house so I managed to persuade Tom to stand outside holding the pumpkin, while I drew him. I loved the way the cold moonlight was in contrast with the warm candlelight. He grumbled a bit after a while as he got cold but we managed to get it done.

River light
Pastel 11 x 16in

The breakfast room
Watercolour & bodycolour
19 x 14in

The morning sun lights up the house in the front and brightens the rooms. Chris is standing at the table but the colours and the patch of light behind her are enough for me to make a painting of it.

Beside the river
Oil 20 x 30in

Alice watching TV
Oil 10 x 14in

This little oil was done one day as Alice sat in her beanbag, favourite teddy and blanket to hand, watching the television. One of the rare occasions any of the children sat still long enough for me to complete a painting.

Sunlight and snow, Taw Valley
Oil 14 x 18in

Taw Valley evening
Oil 14 x 18in

Morning light, Umberleigh
Oil 20 x 24in